WHAT YOUR DOG SAYS ABOUT YOU

HOW YOUR PET'S BREED MATCHES YOUR PERSONALITY

LIAM RYAN

ILLUSTRATIONS BY HUGH FORD

Smith Street Books

CONTENTS

48 Great Dane

50 Greyhound

52 Jack Russell

54 Labrador

56 Lhasa Apso

58 Maltese

60 Mixed Breed

62 Old English Sheepdog

64 Papillon

66 Pomeranian

68 Poodle

70 Portuguese Water Dog

72 Pug

74 Rhodesian Ridgeback

76 Rottweiler

78 Schnauzer

80 Shar Pei

82 Shih Tzu

84 Siberian Husky

86 Staffordshire Terrier

88 St Bernard

90 Weimaraner

92 Yorkshire Terrier

94 Cat

INTRODUCTION

Dogs. They are absolutely bloody everywhere. Whether they're perching in the handbag of a celebrity, rounding up cattle, destroying your bra or pulling a chilly Canadian through a tundra, they play a big part in most cultures on earth. And we have sure come a long way since the days of yore, when wolves busied themselves scaring the crap out of our smelly forebears. We've shifted the bejesus out of that paradigm and now we're firmly in charge.

Oddly, we have chosen to express this dominance over our fluffy allies by undertaking a surreal program of selective breeding. Over the last few millennia this mix and match has left us with dogs available in a mind-boggling range of shapes, sizes, textures and (probably) flavours. You only need to put a bow-wearing Crufts-competing Shih Tzu in the shadow of a Great Dane to realise that we pushed things past ridiculous some time ago.

On top of the obvious physical differences between breeds, this canine explosion has resulted in very specific personality traits. We've got the whole spectrum covered, from aloof independent sorts to excitable pack animals who're so into being part of the family they're online trying to book their place on the annual holiday. With all that choice available, the dog you end up inviting into your home will speak volumes about who you are. So what exactly do you want to say? Let's figure it out.

AFGHAN HOUND

Credited with singlehandedly ushering in the advent of the hair dryer, it is hard to get past the Afghan Hound's fabulous coat. And if you own one, you'd better be enthusiastic about grooming, or prepared to be on a first name basis with Glen from the local poodle parlour. It's the daily grind that makes all the difference. Unbrushed, these dogs look like a drummer in an 80s hair–metal band. Brushed, they look like a mid-90s regional TV newsreader.

Dignified and aristocratic, the breed's distinctive features and coat are a result of its genesis in the Afghan mountains, a place famed for its rugged, brutal climate and fabulous middle-parts.

But there's more to these dogs than a blonde bouffant. One of the oldest breeds in existence and an offshoot of sight hounds, they were originally hunters. In the past they were used to guard sheep and occasionally sent to dispatch large game like deer, wolves, gazelles and, as legend would have it, panthers (!). Some even say this is the breed that Noah took on the ark. Proud owners of the Afghan Hound attest Noah probably wanted something classy knocking about while he was cleaning up after other lesser animals. If you've dedicated yourself to these luscious locks, chances are you have a deep commitment to style and appreciate a touch of the killer instinct.

ALASKAN MALAMUTE

As an owner of this breed, you looove the rugged outdoors or, at the very least, the idea of owning a small part of it. The Alaskan Malamute is as tough as it is fluffy. Kind of like a gobstopper that rolled under the couch years ago, they are hard as nails but soft to the touch. Bred into existence to haul sleds by an Inuit tribe called the Mahlemuts in the barely livable Alaskan wilderness, this breed is an all-terrain unit. Talk of interbreeding with wolves has only bolstered its reputation as a no-nonsense nugget of daring-do. However, your fantasies of having a wolf guard your home are likely to remain just that, as these friendly characters are super happy to pal up with strangers. I guess on the tundra any warm body is a buddy.

Affectionate as these muscle-bound fuzz balls can be, they're also downright stubborn. You need to be an assertive pack leader if you want to avoid the degrading role reversal of being the one wearing the harness as you drag your Malamute to the shops.

But prepare to be willing to let a few things slide, because howling, yard excavation and bin raids brought on by the scavenger instinct are all part of the package.

AUSTRALIAN CATTLE DOG

More Aussie than a meat pie covered in Vegemite and much nicer to look at, the Australian Cattle Dog is a breed born of necessity. Dogs of stamina and endurance, they came into being in the 1800s when moving livestock along hundreds of kilometres of unfenced stock routes proved to be a massive pain in the haunches. So over a span of around 60 years, people chucked a whole bunch of dogs into the mix – even wild dingoes – trying to get the right balance of obedience and desire to nip at sheep and cattle heels (hence the nickname 'heelers').

These guys are fit and robust, and as an owner of this breed you're committing to run the equivalent of a marathon every, let's say, 48 hours, such is the energy of these furry workaholics. But it's not only athletic prowess that the little fellas are known for. They're also hyper intelligent – you just know they have a couple of Rubik's Cubes on the go behind the wool shed. With charges full of brains and brawn, owners of Australian Cattle Dogs are a humble lot. You need to be when you're happy to invite someone cuter, fitter and smarter than you will ever be into your home for life.

BASSET HOUND

As an owner of one of these incomprehensible assemblages of skin, you clearly like a laugh. Things are always funnier with a B-Hound around. Basically they're bloodhounds whose legs got lost in the mail. So here we are with big ol' dogs on tiny little legs — the way it was meant to be. It's not hard to believe that 'bas' is the French word for 'low'. With their baggy skin and droopy eyes, they've got the low vibe covered. Shakespeare even felt moved to describe the modern Bassett Hound's forebears as having 'ears which sweep away the morning dew'. Yes, gravity is greater round a Basset Hound.

If you can believe it, they were bred in the 1800s to hunt and used their formidable sense of smell to track down hares. They can run too, which is a real treat to see — like watching a half-full beanbag in a tumble dryer. Carting round all that excess dermis must be exhausting. Perhaps that's why these guys are such mellow, patient and child-tolerant companions. And as an owner, chances are you're not too wound up either — nobody can take life too seriously with one of these mellow blobs on the end of a lead.

13

BEAGLE

Like your four-legged companion, as a Beagle owner, you like the thrill of the chase. These dogs have a nose for the hunt and so you've got to be A-OK with tracking down your canine pal when she gets caught up in pursuit of a phantom scent. It's a little like living in airport security, but without the rubber gloves or being trapped in the timeless hell of an international terminal.

Looking like Bassett Hounds that didn't order XXL sized skin, Beagles have been depicted in art as far back as Elizabethan times. While dampening a Beagle's desire to track down everything can take some doing, there's a reason they've remained popular for hundreds of years: they are pack animals and will fall head-over-heels in love with their human family. They also don't mind rolling in stinky filth, so look forward to developing Beagle-like olfactory skills to detect whether or not they're too grubby to get on the couch. But you'll probably let them up anyway because you're a kindhearted sucker for big pleading eyes, and Beagles are up the Bambi end of the ocular spectrum. How could anyone resist?! Come on, you stinky adventurer. Up you come.

BICHON FRISE

Let me guess. As an owner of this fluffy breed, you used to dream that your teddy bear would one day come to life. Mission accomplished. You now have in your grasp a fury snow-white pixie with plenty of love to give and plenty of years to give it. Being a smaller dog, a Bichon Frise can live for as long as 20 years. That's a lot of patting time.

With ancestry dating back to the late Middle Ages, these dogs were originally used to tow huge siege towers into place. Ha! Not really. They were doing then what they are doing now: chilling out and taking names. A toy dog first and foremost, the Bichon Frise gained popularity with royal families across Europe, mainly because they were easy to carry and show off (where do you think famed European history scholar Paris Hilton got the idea?). The French and Spanish aristocracy couldn't get enough of them and their popularity was assured by artists like Francisco Goya who crammed them into about 80 per cent of his paintings.

If you have a Bichon in your world, chances are that you also have great spatial awareness, as each step needs to be carefully calculated to avoid landing on your fuzz ball, who just wants to get that tiny bit closer.

BORDER COLLIE

As loved by humans as they are hated by sheep, Collies have energy and brains to burn. Owners of this breed certainly aren't a proud lot — after all, they've had to make peace with the fact that their dog is more intelligent than they are. If you're one of them, you're used to your dog finishing off any cryptic crosswords you've left lying about the place. Generally ranked as the smartest dog breed, Border Collies can comprehend more than 1000 different words — more than you the morning after a big night out. If they don't get enough mental and physical stimulation they can go loopy and use their formidable powers for the forces of evil. Good luck with that.

Hardy and healthy, these Persian sheepdog descendants were bred to thrive along the Scottish–English border. (Look at that! The name totally makes sense.) Don't let their good looks and pretty coat fool you though. These high-octane go-getters are herders first and foremost, and they're here to *work*. You'll need to be cool with seeing everything else you love — other dogs, cats, even children — being herded by a canine that's always on the clock. But at least you have a chum that expects the best from you. What more could you want from a friend? Maybe a moment's peace? Sorry, pal, there's things to do.

BOSTON TERRIER

Goofy is always on the menu with these stump-snouted duffers. If you've got a Boston Terrier, you're most likely the joker of your friendship group. You really have to be up for a laugh when your pooch does this many farts whilst eating, just because it's swallowing so much air. Add to that all the snorting, and you've got audible comedy being blasted from both ends of this furry barrel. Get chuckling or get another dog — these comics are wasted on you.

While the Germans have a fair monopoly when it comes to dog breeding, this is one bulldog extraction born and raised in the US of Aww-look-at that-face. Wide-eyed and famed for being more expressive than a grandpa on a rollercoaster (and indulging in more Kramer-like pratfalls than a dizzy grandpa once he's off that rollercoaster), this energetic terrier has bumbled its way miles from its 19th century origins. Bred to fight yet built to be laughed at, their popularity has risen faster than Tenzing Norgay in a jetpack. On a serious note, with their tendency to overheat they're easier to cook than two-minute noodles, which is the only unfunny thing about them. Ask any owner.

BOXER

Owners of Boxers fancy fitness. You can appreciate good form and athletic prowess, and don't mind watching a little sport. You're certainly no stranger to the odd jog but don't mind that you'll never look as fit as your pooch. This muscle-bound breed, with their perfect posture and proud gait, is as easy to imagine bounding through high grass as working at a standing desk checking in members at a local gym. Fearless, they'd base jump if they could and try to persuade you to come with them.

Bred from Mastiffs and English Bulldogs, they inherited an enviable combination of both parents' agility and strength, but sadly the face and underbite of the latter. Always on the go and not ones to overeat, their very presence in a home implores you to put down that second éclair and go for a run. But they're not the boss of you, so just sit there and watch telly for a minute longer. Chill out, me boundy mate. I went to the gym last week.

BULL TERRIER

When they were handing out pretty, Bull Terriers were at the gym thrashing out bicep curls and squats. Independent and stubborn — like your ex, amirite! — and with a head like a hard-boiled egg with a broken nose (like your ex, amiri— ah forget it) these animals read visually like a cross between a dog and a great white shark. Tough and hardy, their history is a sad one. Blood sports were the drive for creating a dog that has the vice-like jaws of a bulldog mixed with the nimble never-say-die tenacity of a terrier.

Owners of these canines are not about looks, it's what's inside all that muscle that counts. Spirit! You love an underdog, the Rocky Balboa story, the warrior with the heart of gold — because that's what you've got in pooch form. You like walking down the street with an old prizefighter showing him how good life can be outside the ring. The fact that a huge number of Bull Terriers are born deaf only increases the appeal for those who want to see a hero on the canvas get up and face their next challenge.

However, like most of us with a troubled past, Bull Terriers sometimes need a hand working out what's appropriate. Socialisation is the key. Left to its own devices, the breed also does its bit for reinforcing the stereotype of dogs hating cats. That is to say, they get on with cats like cat-murderers and cats. Not fans.

CAVALIER KING CHARLES SPANIEL

Should there be a competition for wankiest name in the animal kingdom, and there really should be, this frilly four-barreled moniker would be hard to beat. Sounding more like an exotic cheese or a B&B you can't afford than a pooch, this breed has enjoyed a long history of royal fandom. King Charles I crushed on the breed big time and before too long every aristocrat worth their ruff wanted one of these doe-eyed bed-warmers in their entourage.

Notable for their big expressive eyes, the CKCS is easy to train and friendlier than that annoying guy at the café who makes small talk about the weather. These little doers love nothing more than hanging with children and will lodge themselves happily in any family.

Having a Cavalier King Charles Spaniel close says that you are someone with a lot of love to give and like to get a return on that investment. You're happy to go with the flow and just see what the day brings, which is a good thing because your flouncy little buddy will just as happily sit on the couch watching Downton Abbey as take in a sedate windy walk. Your choice.

26

CHIHUAHUA

When it comes to teeny tiny dogs, it doesn't get any bigger than this. And ever since Paris Hilton stuffed one of these elves into her handbag, Chihuahua's have been hotter than the Mexican climate their ancestors called home. Small enough to be housed in a Taco shell, their predecessors became an important part of Toltec and Aztec cultures. The tiny companions were sometimes given the dud task of being cremated with their deceased owners to provide protection from evil spirits in the afterlife. I don't want to judge, but it's safe to say that if you're packing a Chihuahua for protection, you haven't thought through your defensive strategy. Nunchucks, sure, but 3 pounds of jittery dog is not going to cut it. But hey, something's gotta burn, right?

Chihuahua is Spanish for 'I swear I left that thing round here somewhere' and owners of this breed love a good game of hide and seek. You're highly evolved when it comes to search and rescue operations, having to investigate hourly the whereabouts of something that is sized appropriately for living in a terrarium but has to fight it out in the real world. Owning one of these also says you're an attentive and careful soul. Allowing yourself one second of inattention would be to squash your mouse-sized chum. You're both protector and destroyer. This is what it is to be a god.

COCKER SPANIEL

Talk about a tail that just won't quit. These suckers love to wag it from sun up to sun down and then some. Cocker Spaniel owners are optimistic types. You don't have a choice because to see a dog like this run up with a ball in its mouth, all floppy and happy, is to see a world full of hope. There are two main types of these big-eared friends: English and American. But for all their differences – the UK version is a bit bigger while the American one has a more domed noggin – both have silky coats, hopeful faces and the haircut of an aunty who still doesn't have her driver's licence. Their name is derived from their 14th century Spanish roots and their appetite for retrieving woodcock – which you'll be relieved to hear is a bird.

Its owners love to love so you can be a bit of a soft touch. Known for their soft pleading eyes and well aware they look fabulous, Cocker Spaniels can be manipulative when they want to be. It's not uncommon for them to use their looks on you to attract bonus snacks. Given the opportunity, they will happily overeat until they turn into big shaggy beanbags, which would be comfortable to sit on but exhausting to groom. And no-one wants to be the owner so negligent that their dog doubles as ridiculous furniture.

CORGI

There's a bit of aristocratic pretension that comes with owning a Corgi. There really shouldn't be as they look pope-on-a-unicycle hilarious, but when – kneels – The Queen – and rises – insists on surrounding herself with Corgis, these things will happen. Originally from Wales ('cor' means 'dwarf' in Welsh), they worked as cattle drovers with what one must assume were the most easily startled cows on earth. Apparently their short stature meant they were harder to kick, so there you go.

The working day has largely ended for the Corgi and it now finds itself a willing chum for play and hangouts. At home, with their low clearance and stumpy legs, it is no surprise that stairs represent a real challenge. Corgi owners either live in a single-storey house or, failing that, they're cool with lugging 25 lb up and down the stairs.

Big brained and adorable, this intelligent breed can pick up tricks darn quickly, and you don't mind showing their skills off to your friends. And if you're anything like your Corgi, you are keen to socialise. But they/you demand a little respect or they/you can get snappy. Which is sort of okay for a stumpy heeler with a height complex, but less cool for a grown-up.

DACHSHUND

Sausage dogs: one of the only mammals capable of being tied into a reef knot, though it is still considered impolite to bend them manually. From Egypt to Mexico there is evidence of Dachshund-like dogs appearing more than 2000 years ago, confirming that the human race is forever linked by our need for oxygen, desire to form social bonds and interest in breeding animals that are 10 times too long for their legs.

Dachshunds are the ice cream of the dog world in that there are heaps of types. Long, smooth and wire haired are all common, with miniature versions of each available. With a modern forebear popping up in the 1400s, the breed's popularity really boomed in the 1800s when the UK and USA went crazy for the German stretch dog. Then the world wars happened, which made Germany and its produce about as cool as a school principal in rollerblades. Sausage dogs have since fought their way back into people's homes and hearts.

Dachshund owners, like their pets, can be aloof because they've already got a best bud who, like, really gets them, you know? They are content to kick back with a good book safe in the knowledge that their dog is so dedicated to them – and only them – that it would read out the passages if it could. Which, let's face it, would be adorable.

DALMATIAN

One thing's for sure, if you're an owner of this breed, you're sick of *101 Dalmatian* jokes. But hey, who isn't? You also like to stand out from the crowd. And even if you don't, too bad, because with this spotty-coated ally at your side you will anyway. Born white, a Dalmatian's distinctive dots appear after a few weeks. Like old Brie cheese, I guess. Over the last 4000 years humans have made this breed work super hard for us. Patrolling borders, hauling carts, herding sheep, delivering pizzas, putting out goddamn fires — their CV is always going to be more impressive than yours.

Bright and outgoing, trained Dalmatians don't mind taking orders and have enough brains and pep to follow through with those commands. After the popularity of those films-that-shall-remain-nameless, quite a few of these high-energy pups ended up in unsuitable homes. Wowed by the cute factor, families didn't realise they had a dog on their hands that could run a marathon without breaking sweat then work an 80-hour week.

It's safe to speculate that nearly all Dalmatian owners have at one time or another considered grabbing a marker and joining the dots to see what it would look like. But then they thought better of it. Because that would be crazy. Cool … but crazy.

37

DOBERMAN PINSCHER

If you were carrying cash and needed an ally to protect you, what breed would you want by your side? If you answered 'Maltese', maybe just stop talking for a while. The correct answer is Doberman. Bred in the late 1800s by a German tax collector who had a heap of cash but even more enemies, this specimen was engineered to be the ultimate in personal protection. Standoffish with strangers, though loyal and smart, this is one breed that will happily follow your orders.

The name 'bitsa' (bits of this, bits of that) would be more appropriate, as these guys are actually a robust mix of Great Dane, Greyhound, Rottweiler, German Shepherd, Pointer and more. Police and war dogs of fearsome reputation, they are strong-willed and motivated, so you need to show them who's boss from an early age to avoid being the one who's ultimately taking orders. As a result, owners of this breed aren't here to mess around. You know what you want and how to get it. You like to give orders and hot damn, do you look good in a uniform.

ENGLISH BULLDOG

Bulldog owners are stoic types, able to weather a storm. Stiff upper-lip. Keep calm and carry on. Spirit of The Blitz and all that jazz. You also don't mind taking care of others. This dense nugget of a dog has been through the mill in terms of breeding and has been left with some, let's say, distinctive characteristics. As a result, health concerns are something owners of these li'l butter balls deal with a lot. Bone problems, eye ailments, eczema. And with heads the size of prize-winning pumpkins, needless to say, they also have trouble giving birth naturally. They've got it all!

With a face only a blind mother could love, they were bred for that unconscionably evil 'sport' bullbaiting. Known for their tenacity, it's said that once a bulldog's jaws latched on, it didn't let go. Weird, then, that now the breed is famed for its patience. They also have a reputation as difficult to train, but you'd be crazy not to put in the hard yards just to see if you can get yours to hold a cigar in its lips and wear a waistcoat so you can take it places dressed as Winston Churchill. This is the dog that will make you look handsome, regardless of how low the bar is to start.

41

FRENCH BULLDOG

Any dog you can imagine wearing a top hat and getting away with it is always going to be popular. So it's no surprise that these squat little chums are now cooler than an iceberg in Ray Bans. So too are the majority of their owners.

Brought into the world in the 1800s when someone had the dog rom-com idea of crossing an English bulldog with a common French ratter, they soon became the go-to pooch for fashionable artists. Little has changed. These little waddlers are now one of the most popular breeds on the planet – rocketing to number four on the US charts, thanks largely to their hipster cred. If you own this breed you are so up with the zeitgeist, you're holding the dog version in your hands.

Not hard to see why. They are pretty adorable. And as if you don't want to get a French Bulldog-sized sidecar to attach to your fixie. But you've got to be a tolerant soul if you own one of these compact li'l buddies – particularly of breathing difficulties and snoring. My god, these little dudes are noisy. If you want something quieter than a sleeping Frenchy at the foot of your bed, just fire up a cement mixer and fill it with snooker balls.

GERMAN SHEPHERD

Now everyone will take you seriously. The dog of choice for law enforcement and despotic regimes the world over, German Shepherds are not here to mess around. Owners of these dogs probably don't like to talk to strangers and if they have to they at least want them to be a little scared.

Wolf-like in appearance and with a bark like an 18th century cannon, these loyal and curious creatures have their roots in Germany (obvs). Originally herders, the Alsatian has since graduated to search-and-rescue, police and military roles. The promotion is no surprise considering they are intelligent, easy to train, motivated, and can strip and reassemble most standard issue firearms in a combat setting.

German Shepherd owners are practical and probably look damn good in a uniform. You are also confident folk, safe in the knowledge that you've won the trust of your no-nonsense dog and will get to live another day. You also have a lot of free time because this dog demands exercise and regular engagement, or else it will use that massive brain to find new and destructive ways to assert itself. Game on.

45

GOLDEN RETRIEVER

Gold in colour and gold medals for temperament! This upbeat breed seems to have been engineered in a lab to be the perfect addition to a family. Owners of these dogs like a good smile and are content in the knowledge that they're guaranteed picture-perfect family portraits worthy of the opening credits of an 80s sitcom. Yes, these dogs are as easy to please as they are playful, which has made them among the most popular breeds in the UK, USA and Australia. They are also popular assistance dogs. Damned over achievers.

Bred in Scotland in the mid-1800s as gun dogs to fetch slaughtered animals from both land and ponds — they were just happy to be involved, really! — today they are still super keen to, well, retrieve things. With their mouth. So its masters need to have developed some degree of patience during the early years of ownership as they got used to having all their worldly possessions passed through the maw of a housemate with the dopey expression of one just struck on the head with a roofing tile.

Bottom line, owners of these dogs need to be happy-go-lucky because being sad next to a Golden Retriever looks absolutely ridiculous.

46

GREAT DANE

Sure, deep down, owners of this breed really wanted a horse. To own a Great Dane is to share in a slice of ancient history, with early kin of the breed depicted on the walls of ancient Egyptian tombs. When its ancestors plodded onto the scene somewhere between 3000 BC and the late Jurassic, the hunting game changed. Humans had at their disposal a beast bigger than most that could help fell gigantic creatures. From boars to bears, we could hunt them all!

However, things didn't quite stay that way when these gentle giants eventually proved themselves more adept at chilling out and receiving pats than chasing and killing. Their docile nature is a blessing for their owners, who are trusting types. However, you know it would take mere seconds of inattention for something that size to Hulk out and Maramaduke your house into a flat-pack of carnage. A Great Dane currently holds the dog height record with the aptly named Zeus maxing out at 112 cm/44 inches from paw to shoulder. Now that's an animal that could flip a Honda if it hit it at the right angle. You know the risk, and society trusts you won't weaponise your friendly Godzilla and start invading neighbouring states.

49

GREYHOUND

If you've invited one of these slim-hipped slumber machines into your life, it's likely that you don't mind putting the ol' feet up. In fact, Greyhound owners have probably watched more Netflix than their friends combined because their fury friends get an A+ for chilling out. Greyhounds have been much loved for millennia, simultaneously winning hearts and breaking land-speed records since 4000 BC. But for dogs that can clock a hectic 60 km/ 37 miles per hour on foot and have Usain Bolt-like levels of fast twitch muscle, they are adept couch potatoes, regularly racking up a narcoleptic 18 hours of sleep a day.

As a lot of these pooches are ex-racing dogs, it's easy to see why they're more than happy to squander their talents, catch ZZZs and soak up the love — they've been through the mill and know how good they now have it. And as a proud owner, you'll take any opportunity to tell people that you do too. If driving a conversation back to talking about your dog was an Olympic sport you'd probably win gold.

JACK RUSSELL

As a Jack Russell owner, you need to have your wits about you, or there's every chance they'll outfox you quicker than you can say, 'Why am I making this dog brunch?'. These fearless tykes were cooked up by a Reverend Russell (get it?) some 200 years ago to chase down game without killing it. This means they get bored easily, so you'd better find activities for them that are at least as engaging as chasing a rabbit down a burrow. Which can be difficult in an apartment.

Super motivated, energetic and totally into everything, they are one of the toughest breeds padding around. And like a little tough guy after six pints, they may snap to prove it. You're probably pretty proud of yourself for living harmoniously with a Jack Russell. You took the challenge and won! But if you haven't bothered to train your little Rambo, it'll take five seconds of boredom for this dog to hide the remote or dig a swimming pool-sized hole in the yard. Trained, they'll pretty much reply to your questions in full sentences. Sure, a talking dog would be a real feather in the cap in terms of your discipline and application. But annoying when they inevitably start having an opinion about what movie you're going to stream.

53

LABRADOR

Labradors are one of the most loved and photographed breeds on the planet. In fact, they are the most popular dogs in the UK, USA, and Australia. Yet no-one has ever uttered the words 'I've seen too many Labradors – I'm over it!'. That's just never going to happen. Friendly, full of life and coming in gold, chocolate and black, they have everything you could want in a human friend, with better hair.

The breed originated on Newfoundland in the 17th century when fishermen got sick of retrieving nets and the like from the icy water. They then earned their stripes as gun dogs and have been helping people ever since. Now they fill the majority of assistance roles, with Golden Retrievers and German Shepherds a distant second and third. Better behaved than you are (and certainly more employable), the Labrador has earned a reputation as the perfect family pet.

Owning a Labrador suggests you are an enthusiastic type who is keen to see what fresh fun is around the next corner. Because when your dog is the poster child for positive psychology and up for pretty much anything, you have to meet them halfway. Otherwise you look a curmudgeon. Even if that's the case, your Lab will love you all the same. They're good like that. Plus, they know you provide all the food and they will seriously devour anything. If you put peanut butter on a whole raw pumpkin, these furry-gourmands would probably gobble it down.

LHASA APSO

Emerging from Tibet, this little dog with 4000 years of traceable history could have done with a career guidance counsellor. Although Tibetan Mastiffs patrolled the outside of Tibetan monasteries, these mini sentinels were bred to alert the monks to any intruders that made it inside. It was probably assumed that by the time an intruder made it past the gigantic mastiffs they would need little more than a shrill bark to think 'Screw this, let's hit up that place across the valley'.

Don't let the blow wave fool you because the guard dog habit has been a hard one to kick. To this Lhasa Apsos retain their keen sense of hearing (in fact, they can take blindness in their stride) and tend to be wary of strangers. They also score pretty average on dog intelligence scales but that doesn't stop them strutting around like they own the joint, filling what can be 20-plus years of life running a protection detail for their owners. Owners of this little breed are patient types who can tolerate those who have delusions of grandeur. But as cocky and yappy as these little upstarts may be, it's all done to protect their number-one asset: you. Which is nice.

MALTESE

Owners of these fabulous little lushes don't mind pampering. You also fancy yourself as a hairdresser. Or at least a shearer. Because if you're neither of those things, you'll be forced to hack your way out of the fur tendrils that have ensnared you from a growing coat that just won't quit. Yes, the hair on this tiny breed grows so fast one can safely assume there is a gypsy curse at work. Groomed with a long coat, they tend to look like a drag queen's wig with eyes stuck on. Unsocialised, they can act like tiny drama queens, yapping away and demanding attention.

The Maltese is a dog that was built for the high life. Coming from Malta with a history stretching back to Roman times, this breed (like many toy dogs) became hugely popular with royalty. Living with the top tier, they often slept in their owners' beds and were carried round in the pockets of puffy garments. Much loved, they attracted many names including the Roman Ladies' Dog and one coined by someone who had never seen a jungle cat in their lives that translates to Maltese Lion Dog. Owners of this breed like to give — be it pats, snacks or general attention. And you are in luck because your Maltese friend here sure as hell likes to receive all of the above. Often while lying down. It's tiring staying this marvellous.

MIXED BREED

Purebreds are often engineered through arranged 'marriages' where offspring are drawn from genetic pools so small they make the royal family's stock look like the Pacific Ocean. But mixed breed dogs (as distinct from mutts) represent breeding more the way nature intended it: not between cousins. Often prompted by attempts to get a 'designer dog' by mixing certain breeds' desirable traits: a Great Dane's size and a Dachshund's legs? Sure, why not? Bull Terrier face and Chihuahua size? Cool! Pomeranian fluff and a Poodle's fluff? So. Much. Fluff! Sometimes, though, the blending is the result of less-than-robust fencing when nature — ahem — runs its course!

Typified by their portmanteau names (Labrador + Poodle = Labradoodle), mixed-breed dogs will often avoid many of the health problems that some purebreds endure as a result of their incestuous origins. However, over-enthusiastic blending to get a certain look can cause its fair share of problems too.

Mixed breed owners are the type of people who know what they like and don't mind hunting around to get it. What you want's not available? No drama, you'll make your own. You also like rolling the dice because with some mixed breeds it's anybody's guess what the cocktail will produce. And, unlike a beverage, it may take more than a little umbrella to make it palatable.

OLD ENGLISH SHEEPDOG

'Get a haircut', you might yell to one of these furry friends if you were out of work with a bit of time to kill. But this friendly Wookie wouldn't care. They are happy-go-lucky types with energy to burn. With their iconic coats and eyes obscured by hair, it is thought that Old English Sheepdogs invented bangs.

The name is a bit of a lie – the breed isn't, all things considered, that old. Emerging in the mid 18th century, these fluff balls were terrific at driving sheep to market. On foot, not behind the wheel. Though this is certainly a dog one can imagine behind the wheel of a lorry, like a big adorable Muppet in a flat-cap, taking care of business.

In terms of demeanour, these dogs tend to be goofy extroverts who are super social and able to adapt to different environments. As a sheep dog owner, you probably tend to like to go with the flow too and have a bit of fun while you're at it. You're up for a quick beer or wine but you're also ready if someone arrives with some harebrained idea to play mini golf while wearing a silly hat. You could also be forgiven for harbouring fantasies of one day embarking on a big adventure, with your goofy furry sidekick as co-pilot, like Han Solo.

PAPILLON

Don't mention the ears. Because this Spock-headed dude is bound to hear it. The name is derived from the French for 'butterfly', and once you see its ear-wings you can't un-see them. Fast fact: the drop-eared version is called a Phalène, which translates to 'moth'. This seems to suggest that the French are as obsessed with dogs ears as they are with good wine, great cheese and providing tourists with curt service.

The first evidence of the breed comes from Italy around 700 years ago, when painters loved putting them on canvas in the arms of fancy ladies. Over time, they burrowed their way into French folklore. Rumour has it, Marie Antoinette carried one with her on the way to the guillotine. It was probably a last-ditch effort to see if the executioner would accept a canine proxy for the de-noggining.

The Papillon has a thin fox-like nose, tiny head and fine bones. It's self-confident, brainy and good at tricks. When it stares at you, it looks like it can hear your thoughts. Owners of this breed like the finer things in life. Fine music, fine-boned dogs, fine French wines. You're sensitive to all the beauty that is out there. Particularly if it's in audio form.

65

POMERANIAN

Just stop. This thing is more ridiculous than carrying a leg of ham in a BabyBjörn. Also known as the 'Pom', no doubt for its resemblance to the fluffy cheering aid, the pompom, the Pomeranian is a shrinking absurdity. Drawn from the Pomeranian region of Central Europe, these dogs represent what happens when humans spend centuries trying to miniaturise an Alaskan Malamute. Over time, the Pomeranian has been bred down into smaller and smaller sizes. In her lifetime, super-fan Queen Victoria even oversaw a reduction in size of about 50 per cent through selective breeding. That's the genetic equivalent of putting an empty packet of crisps in the oven to shrink. At this stage, the process should reach its logical conclusion in 2115 AD, when Pomeranians become the size of cotton buds. Yapping cotton buds. It's all we've ever wanted!

With a sidekick known for its pluck, excitability and fur that makes it seem to be forever passing through an electrical storm, keeping a Pomeranian close suggests you have a taste for the absurd and are adept at handling life's curveballs with a wry smile.

Despite the boofiness, Pomeranians are actually remarkably sturdy. They must know they are durable because they'll tend to strut round like they own the place. Which is pretty remarkable considering they can fit in a regulation coffee cup.

POODLE

Throughout history, overzealous groomers have done their best to turn this breed into walking topiary. With its prance and primp it may look pretentious; however, this breed is totally cool to hang out with, enjoys meeting new people and is eager to please. As a poodle owner, you like taking the easy way round but don't mind looking good while you're at it. You may also have a sensitive constitution but at least with these hypoallergenic (and relatively odourless) comrades you can get away with it.

Thought to have been brought to France from Germany in the 1400s, the breed's good nature and aesthetic potential obviously clicked with the French, and its popularity boomed. As a mark of respect, you shouldn't be above dropping the odd French phrase for the benefit of your Poodle.

Like a friend you'd want to have a few drinks with, Poodles are sensitive souls with knockout haircuts who respond well to your vocal tone. Obviously regular haircuts are necessary, and depending on the cut and colour, the look can land anywhere between late-80s Cher and a snow drift. Bonne chance!

PORTUGUESE WATER DOG

Portuguese. Water. Dog. The name has it all. Something fluffy. Something necessary for our survival. And a place we know nothing about. While excelling at colonial expansion, someone in Portugal also found time to look at dogs and think, 'I bet we can make that float'. And they did. Bred to help fishermen with their catch, these guys boomed in popularity along the Portuguese coast.

Traditionally their hindquarters are shaved to aid swimming while the rest of their coat is left black and curly. This tends to leave groomed specimens looking a lot like Slash from Guns N' Roses after losing his board shorts at a pool party.

If you're an owner of a Portuguese Water Dog, chances are you're a bit of a Barack Obama: a self-assured leader with a strong decision-making game. The US President — AKA the most powerful person on earth apart from Bono — has deemed this pooch worthy of living at the White House. You should feel secure in the knowledge that one of these dogs is closer to the nuclear launch codes than most of the US military's top brass. Just don't catch anyone calling your hound a poodle. You hate that!

PUG

If you're a pug owner, chances are you hate being surprised. It's one of the main reasons you got your hands on this respiratorily-challenged snorter. As the time-honoured saying goes, 'You can always hear a Pug coming'. But secretly you don't really mind — all that honking drowns out issues arising from your own sleep apnoea.

With their big bone structure, wrinkly skin, curled tail and bulgy black eyes peering out of a crushed-Coke-can-of-a-face, Pugs give us pause to consider how far dogs have evolved from wolves. They were originally bred in China and brought to Europe in the 16th century where, like nice fabrics and cousin seduction, they became popular with the aristocracy. And their popularity boomed, driven by their reputation as peppy and animated companions with big personalities and sensitive hearts.

Maybe too sensitive. Pugs are susceptible to all kinds of ailments, from rashes and colds to brain swelling. As a pug owner, chances are you're a wannabe doctor with a medicine cabinet so well stocked it would rival a small pharmacy. You're also a calorie counting zealot, because a little overfeeding will transform an already barrel-like pug into a Zeppelin. And weight gain promotes more wheezing and snoring. The result? A companion whose breathing sounds like a pig drinking custard. No-one wants that.

73

RHODESIAN RIDGEBACK

In terms of difficulty, this is the black diamond run of dog ownership. When you take one these powerful giants into your home, you're taking on something bred to track and chase lions. Literally. Emerging in South Africa from the wild dog stock that gives the breed its unique ridge, Rhodesian Ridgebacks can run for 30 miles without tiring. It's not just the punk Mohawk fur-cut that suggests they don't give a stuff; they have the tough gung-ho attitude to back it up and they know no fear.

No-one should be shocked to hear that a lion-chasing animal with wild dog heritage needs a whole heap of exercise. Owners of Rhodesian Ridgebacks love a challenge. And when your dog is able to look a lion in the eyes as easily as it can chase a ball, as a Rhodesian Ridgeback owner you're going to have to bring bucket-loads of charisma and authority to the training table. But anything's possible when you own a Ridgeback. You're the kind of individual who can look at nature in all its rugged unpredictability and think, 'Yeah, I can tame that. See? I already have.'

ROTTWEILER

Boy, do these dudes get some bad press. I mean, you kill a few people and — BAM — everyone's afraid. But Rotty owners don't care what everyone thinks. As an owner of this bulky breed, you're aware that there will be some people that think your hellhound will rip your head off (literally) if you give it half a chance. But you know the bad press is wrong, dammit! These loping canines have hearts of gold. And they're oh-so pretty too. With their black coats and tan booties Rottweilers would look as good on the catwalks of Milan as they do pinning a would-be burglar against the fence of a warehouse.

The history of Rottweilers is shrouded in mystery but it's thought they were used by Roman legions to guard livestock and probably scare soon-to-be conquered nations into opening the gates. Despite their fearsome reputation they have maintained their popularity to this day, partially because it is pretty easy and hilarious to imagine them wearing a soldier's helmet and starring in their own action film.

Owners tend to be the kind of people to stick up for a mate because they really value loyalty. It's a quality that can't be measured, but if we could, it would max out at this 60 kg/130 lb of furry muscle. Strong and powerful, Rottweilers look like they could bench 130 kg/300 lb and run through a wall before breakfast. But who wants any of that destructive chaos when they can get love and pats from their human?

SCHNAUZER

This breed is known for their old-man-ish salt-and-pepper hairstyle, big-beard and super-bushy eyebrows. It's a look that screams 'Hey, you kids! Get off my lawn' and 'Where did I put my glasses?'. It fits the demeanour of these protective allies. Friendly and fiercely loyal to those they know and wary of anyone unknown entering their patch, they are the loving grandparents of the dog world.

The Schnauzer originated in Germany in the 15th century, where it is known by the very-yellable name Mittelschnauzer! They were bred as ratters but then proved themselves as guard dogs with a bark far bigger than their bite, and were even adept at delivering messages during times of war.

Schnauzer owners know what they like, so let's keep it that way, thank you very much. Your house is your castle and intruders need to pass muster. That's where these little buddies come into their own. They'll run a tight border patrol at your front door so you can keep things the way you want. Good dog. You totally get it.

SHAR PEI

Famed for their folds of skin and permanently furrowed expressions, these corrugated snorting nuggets appear to carry the weight of the world more than most. But as they were once considered a legitimate menu item, you can forgive them for looking a little moody. Bred in China as guard dogs and then used as fighters, Shar Peis were once considered a delicacy but have fortunately since moved off the dining table and into the home proper.

While as puppies with those ridiculous skin rolls they're the cutest things on planet earth (FACT), as adults they can be stubborn, crave attention and be prone to ailments. Yes, on paper they really do seem to be a handful. Territorial and not for novice owners, Shar Peis often loathe water with the fire of a thousand suns, can give first-time patters a weird rash, are prone to eye and skin problems, and can take a heap of time to socialise. Sort of like that weird kid at school with allergies and tinted glasses who ate nothing but cheese sticks.

But owners of this breed know that beauty is only wrinkly-skin deep. You know what you're into and stick with your choices. You understand that stubbornness is just another form of passion and that there's zero chance of your loyal little chubster ever seeking greener pastures elsewhere. Good work, me chunky little chum.

SHIH TZU

The Tibetan breeder who first set their mind to bringing this hirsute pygmy into existence sure must have had a sense of humour. There is no funnier dog name, and few canines look as hilarious. Shih Tzu owners are likely to be into pretty things. A theory based mainly on the fact it's hard to imagine this breed outside a living room filled with a staggering amount of throw pillows and some gold filigree. They are also into a bit of mystery, because the jury's still out on what exactly a Shih Tzu looks like underneath all that fur.

Owners also consider an independent nature to be a virtue. Maybe you actually just wanted a cat. Because while affectionate and playful, this fuzz ball can act like a teenager that is totally over your s#%t and just wants to do its own thing. You also need to be keen groomers to avoid ending up living in a fantastical forest made entirely of your pet's fur. Plus, all it takes is a little brushing and snipping to make your dog look like a miniature Texan beauty queen crossed with a Wookie. The dream.

SIBERIAN HUSKY

Tilt your head back and howl at the moon because this is where things get wild. An animal born of necessity in the icy hell that is Siberia, the Husky earned its chops (literally) by dragging the locals on sleds from one inconceivable hardship to another. The breed then became legendary in America around 1925 when a team of sled dogs led by Balto saved the town of Nome from disease by delivering an essential serum.

As a result of this great press and being as cuddly as they are durable, Huskies sometimes find themselves in inappropriate homes where misguided owners figure this Wolf Lite will like nothing more than to cuddle up on the couch in the tropics. Wrong. With their strong-padded feet, dense coat and alien-like metabolism, Huskies are suited to conditions so hostile they make your freezer feel like the Bahamas.

Husky owners like the sweet taste of adventure, a raised pulse and having a wide horizon to explore. Wherever you roam, you know you'll have an ally who will be with you every step of the way — completely un-puffed and ready for more. And more. And more! If this gets a little much, you always have the option to rig up a sled so your indefatigable buddy can drag you to the shops. Produce aisle. MUSH!

85

STAFFORDSHIRE TERRIER

Who wants to own a tiny seal with legs? Everyone? Good, because that's pretty much the Staffy look. A mix of bulldog and terrier with a bit of leopard seal dusted in, these wedge-headed dogs were originally bred in the 1800s for bull baiting. As much as they were brought into the world to fight, now all they really want to do is fight to win your love. Noted for their loyalty, these little nuggets are sensitive souls who will buy into their family unit lock, stock and barrel.

They do their best work by their owner's side so will always want to be included in any plans that may be in the offing. But maybe don't take them to the dog park — they're just not that into other canines, if you get my drift. Staffy owners are social types who like company, even if their main companion is the four-legged variety. Because the best experiences in life are those that are shared. And you'll share everything with this loved-up friend because they will always want to be super close.

Fearless and affectionate in equal measure, this is a dog that likes adventure as much as sitting uncomfortably close as you chill out watching Netflix.

ST BERNARD

The iconic image of the St Bernard is of the big fella charging through the snow with a barrel on his collar to provide life-giving booze to those lost in the cold. Some call that heroism, others reckless negligence in providing a blood-thinning agent to those with a core temperature so low it could kill them. You don't want to call a dog a murderer but here we are. So if you fancy a tipple, you're the type to keep a St Bernard close. Or far, for that matter. Distance isn't an issue, because when it comes to providing a beverage with a kick, these guys live to deliver to your liver. They're the most bear-like of bartenders this side of your local gay pub.

In the 1700s the Swiss were tired of rescuing people along the Great St Bernard Pass so brought these chunky workers onto the payroll. Excelling at herding, guarding, eating and rescuing, they are mountain dogs through and through — in both origin and size. Yes, there's no easy way to say it, but St Bernard's are chunky — some weighing in at 120 kg/265 lb. Fortunately they're docile. If they weren't they would pretty much be in charge of Switzerland right now instead of following you round with booze. Party on, Bernie! Mine's a double.

WEIMARANER

A big dog used to hunt big game, the Weimaraner is a goofy-looking predator that was bred in the 1800s to do the dangerous food acquisition jobs no-one else wanted to do. Once humans got rid of most of the big game in Europe (your move, nature), the popularity of this monochrome ally slipped away. But they have made a resurgence, showing they can hang with humans as well as they can murder terrified beasts.

Named after the Weimar Republic of their origin, they're super smart and gifted with a keen sense of smell. They are also prodigious runners able to cover huge amounts of territory without fatigue. Were they human, they'd be those annoying people who try to maintain a conversation while jogging. The worst.

Weimeraner owners are active and don't mind being round Type A personalities. They are drawn to those go-getters who will book a holiday on a whim or decide to run a half-marathon next weekend because YOLO. A Weimaraner will typically act like a puppy long into adulthood and find it hard to suppress its instinct to hunt and kill. As a result, owners are adept at smiling and shaking their heads as if to say 'classic Weimaraner' as yet another terrified cat rockets over the fence to escape certain death.

YORKSHIRE TERRIER

Like so many of humanity's greatest inventions, the Yorkshire Terrier was created to kill rats. Most of which would have been of an equal size to this teeny pooch, which makes it the meanest thing you can carry round in a coffee mug. Straddling the line between toy and terrier dog, Yorkies show scant regard for weight class and will adorably act like they can take on anything from a Rottweiler to a Sherman tank (which would be pretty cute if you could get over the fact a tank had rolled into your backyard).

For something that was bred to slaughter vermin in the 1800s, they have enjoyed a meteoric rise in social class. Now many of the breed have moved on to be groomed and pampered within an inch of their dignity.

Fiercely territorial and adept at snuggling, they can switch faster from 'I could sit in front of this fire snoozing forever' to 'I will use all 2 kg/4 lb of my ferocity to destroy this intruder for you, master' than most breeds. Yorkie owners don't like getting pushed around and they certainly have no qualms boxing above their weight. You like and respect a bit of pluck, especially when it comes in an adorable fury package that can really rock a scrunchie.

CAT

As a cat owner, you will definitely die alone.

Published in 2016 by Smith Street Books
Melbourne | Australia
smithstreetbooks.com

ISBN: 9781925418019

CIP data is available from the National Library of Australia.

Publisher: Paul McNally
Design and Illustration: Hugh Ford
Editor: Davina Bell

Printed & bound in China by C&C Offset Printing Co., Ltd.

Book 13
10 9 8 7 6 5 4 3 2 1